I Want to Be a
GREAT WHITE
SHARK

by Thomas Kingsley Troupe

illustrated by Stephanie Boey

A crowd stood near the railing on the deck of a cruise ship. People stared out at the ocean waves.

"What's everyone looking at, Rosa?" asked my little brother, George.

"It's a great white shark," I said. "See him out there?"

"Wow," George whispered.

The shark swam out of sight, and we hurried towards the swimming pool. It was really crowded.

"I want to be a great white shark," I said. "Then people would get out of my way!"

Don't ask me how it happened, but it did. I became a great white shark! I swam through the water and scared everyone. I could have the whole pool to myself!
But the water didn't feel right, so I dove deeper.

Suddenly the pool was gone, and I was swimming in the ocean. It was my new home.

Soon my shark tummy rumbled. I was so hungry!
Where can a shark find a sandwich?

"Hungry, are you?" said an older great white.
He swam closer and introduced himself. His name
was Jack.

"What do we eat?" I asked.

"Let's eat a seal," he said.

"What?" I asked. "Do we have to?"

"That's what we sharks do!"

"Go after that one!" he shouted.

I wanted to show this shark that I knew what I was doing. The seal shot across the water. I sped after him and snapped my jaws.

"Aw, you missed," Jack moaned.

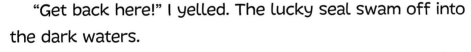

"Get back here!" I yelled. The lucky seal swam off into the dark waters.

"Let's try something smaller," Jack said.

I followed him towards a school of fish. We hungrily ate them up!

Great white sharks often hunt seals, but they also eat fish, squid and stingrays. After a really big feed, a shark can go for up to one month before eating again.

I was huge! My shark body was about as long as my dad's pickup truck. I weighed about as much too. Even so, I swam through the ocean with ease. Breathing through gills felt strange, but I didn't have to go up to the surface for air.

My big mouth made a deadly weapon. It felt like I had hundreds of little knives for teeth! Amazingly, though, when one fell out, another grew in its place.

A great white shark's teeth are serrated. That means they are rough like a saw. An average great white shark tooth is about the size of a triangular tortilla crisp.

"I smell something strange," I said. "I think I like it."

"Probably blood," Jack said. "We can smell blood from 1.6 kilometres (1 mile) away."

"I didn't even know blood had a smell," I said.

This might sound crazy, but it smelled as delicious as bread baking in the oven.

As if my super sniffer wasn't enough, I could hear EVERYTHING in the ocean. With my small shark ears I could hear fish swimming and seals thrashing.

"Whoa!" I said. "It's like I've got shark superpowers."

Sharks use electroreception to help them hunt prey. When a creature moves, it gives off small electrical currents. Sharks have pores on their faces that pick up those currents. Electroreception helps sharks to home in on their prey with DEADLY accuracy.

We swam towards the shore. A few other
sharks had also gathered there. They were
looking at legs – human legs – in the water.

"Okay, there's no way I'm eating humans," I said. "Fish? Yes. Seals? Maybe."

I was hungry, but not that hungry.

"Don't worry," Jack said. "We don't usually bite humans. I hear they taste awful!"

Sharks rarely attack humans. In 2014, there were only three deadly shark attacks in the world. In fact, there's more chance of being struck by lightning than being attacked by a shark.

Swimming with the big sharks made me forget about swimming with the other boys and girls back on the cruise ship. Then a little shark swam close by.

"Hey, little one," I said. "Where's your mum?"

The little shark smiled. He already had lots of teeth!

"Great white pups are born with teeth," Jack said. "Baby sharks come from eggs inside the mother shark. The eggs hatch inside the mother, and the babies gobble up any extra eggs."

"Eggs are delicious, but that's disgusting," I said.

"They have to eat something," Jack said.

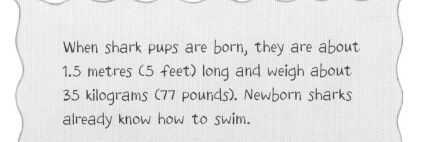

When shark pups are born, they are about 1.5 metres (5 feet) long and weigh about 35 kilograms (77 pounds). Newborn sharks already know how to swim.

Later I spotted some sharks with scars all over their bodies.

"Wow," I said. "You look tough."

"Tough?" one of them said. "I've just been around a long time. I'm almost 60 years old. "

Although no one knows for sure, scientists believe great white sharks can live for up to 70 years or more!

"Always fighting for food isn't easy," one shark said. "You can get pretty beaten up."

"Poachers are the worst," the other said. "They hunt and kill sharks for our jaws, teeth and fins."

"That's horrible!" I gasped. "I always thought humans were afraid of sharks, not the other way around."

Soon I heard familiar voices calling my name. I said goodbye to my shark friends and swam back towards the ship. I felt my body changing back to its human form. I swam to the surface, and I was in the pool once again.

"I'm starving," George said. "Is it time for lunch?"

"Good idea," I said. "Can we have fish fingers?"

"You don't like fish," Mum said.

"I do now!" I said with a grin.

Great white sharks are incredible predators. But they
are under threat from illegal hunting around the world.
Conservation groups have worked to keep great white sharks
from becoming extinct. Because of such work, the number of
great white sharks is growing in many areas.

More about great white sharks

• Great white sharks are the largest predatory fish on Earth.

• Sharks have large brains — among the largest of any animal when compared to its body size.

• Many sharks can roll their eyes back into their sockets for protection.

• Some sharks can burst out of the water and become completely airborne.

Glossary

accuracy being free of mistakes

conservation protection of animals and plants, as well as looking after the natural environment

electrical current flow of electricity

electroreception ability to detect electrical currents; some fish have sensory organs that give them this ability

extinct no longer living; an extinct animal is one that has died out, leaving no more of its kind

fin body part that fish use to swim and steer in water

gills body part on the side of a fish; sharks use their gills to breathe

poacher person who hunts or fishes illegally

predator animal that hunts other animals for food

prey animal hunted by another animal for food

Read more

Shark (DK Eyewitness), Miranda Macquitty (DK Children, 2011)

Shark vs Penguin (Predator vs Prey), Mary Meinking Chambers (Raintree, 2012)

Shocking Sharks (Walk on the Wild Side), Charlotte Guillain (Raintree, 2013)

Websites

www.bbc.co.uk/nature/life/Great_white_shark
Find out more about great white sharks.

www.ngkids.co.uk/did-you-know/great_white_sharks
Ten fascinating facts about great white sharks.

Index

Books in this series

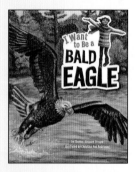
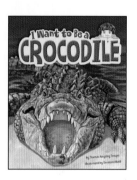

Raintree is an imprint of Capstone Global Library Limited, a company incorporated in England and Wales having its registered office at 7 Pilgrim Street, London, EC4V 6LB – Registered company number: 6695582

www.raintree.co.uk
myorders@raintree.co.uk

Text © Capstone Global Library Limited 2016
The moral rights of the proprietor have been asserted.

Edited by Shelly Lyons and Nick Healy
Designed by Sarah Bennett
Creative Director: Nathan Gassman
Production by Tori Abraham

ISBN 978 1 4747 0421 2
19 18 17 16 15
10 9 8 7 6 5 4 3 2 1

British Library Cataloguing in Publication Data
A full catalogue record for this book is available from the British Library.

Acknowledgements
The illustrator would like to dedicate this book to Oh Shen Li – S.B.

The illustrations in this book were created with coloured pencil. The photographs on pages 20–21 are reproduced with permission of: Shutterstock/Fiona Ayerst

We would like to thank Christopher G. Lowe, PhD, for his expterise, research and advice.

Every effort has been made to contact copyright holders of material reproduced in this book. Any omissions will be rectified in subsequent printings if notice is given to the publisher.

All the internet addresses (URLs) given in this book were valid at the time of going to press. However, due to the dynamic nature of the internet, some addresses may have changed, or sites may have changed or ceased to exist since publication. While the author and publisher regret any inconvenience this may cause readers, no responsibility for any such changes can be accepted by either the author or the publisher.

Printed in China.